Our World

Rivers and Lakes

By Kate Bedford

Aladdin/Watts

PAPERBACK EDITION PRINTED 2007

© Aladdin Books Ltd 2006

Designed and produced by
Aladdin Books Ltd
2/3 Fitzroy Mews
London W1T 6DF

First published in 2006 by
Franklin Watts
338 Euston Road
London NW1 3BH

Franklin Watts Australia
Level 17/207 Kent Street
Sydney NSW 2000

Franklin Watts is a division of
Hachette Children's Books

ISBN 978 0 7496 7756 5

A catalogue record for this
book is available from the
British Library.

Dewey Classification:
577.6

Editor:
Harriet Brown

Designer:
Flick, Book Design and Graphics

Picture researcher:
Alexa Brown

Literacy consultant:
Jackie Holderness – former Senior
Lecturer in Primary Education,
Westminster Institute,
Oxford Brookes University

Printed in Malaysia

Photocredits:

Abbreviations: l-left, r-right, b-bottom, t-top,
c-centre, m-middle
Front cover – Photodisc. Back cover –
Secretaría de turismo, Argentina.
03bl, 15mr, 16tl, 19tr, 25tl, 28tl, 30tr –
Corbis, 03ml, 04bl, 08br, 10br, 15tl, 16br,
21tr, 21br, 23br, 28bl, 29tr, 31bl – Corel,
18tl, 19bl, 25br – Digital Vision, 22bl, 23mr
– Flat Earth, 13bl – John Foxx Images, 29mc
– NASA's Earth Observatory, 2-3, 04tl, 08tl,
13tl, 14tl, 14br, 17tl, 17mr, 23tr, 24tr, 24bl,
27tr, 30mr, 31tl – Photodisc, 11tl – Select
Pictures, 20tr – Flick Smith, 03tl, 06tr, 06bl,
09tl, 10tl, 12tr, 12bl, 22tl, 30br – Stockbyte,
18br - www.istockphoto.com / Bill Storage,
26bl – www.istockphoto.com / Chris Schmidt,
20bl - www.istockphoto.com / Dolph
Mathews, 27bl – www.istockphoto.com / PJ
Macchia, 26tr – www.istockphoto.com /
Stuart Blyth

CONTENTS

Notes to parents and teachers

This series has been developed for group use in the classroom as well as for children reading on their own. In particular, its differentiated text allows children of mixed abilities to enjoy reading about the same topic. The larger size text (A, below) offers apprentice readers a simplified text. This simplified text is used in the introduction to each chapter and in the picture captions. This font is part of the © Sassoon family of fonts recommended by the National Literacy Early Years Strategy document for maximum legibility. The smaller size text (B, below) offers a more challenging read for older or more able readers.

A river's journey

Many rivers begin on high ground in the mountains where there is lots of rain and snow. Rivers flow downhill.

A

◄ This stream begins at a spring.

The place where a river begins is called its source. The source is sometimes a spring.

B

Questions, key words and glossary

Each spread ends with a question which parents and teachers can use to discuss and develop further ideas and concepts. Further questions are provided in a quiz on page 30. A reduced version of pages 30 and 31 is shown below. The illustrated 'Key words' section is provided as a revision tool, particularly for apprentice readers, in order to help with spelling, writing and guided reading as part of the literacy hour. The glossary is for more able or older readers. In addition to the glossary's role as a reference aid, it is also designed to reinforce new vocabulary and provide a tool for further discussion and revision. When glossary terms first appear in the text they are highlighted in bold.

 See how much you know!

What happens to lakes and rivers during a drought?

Can you name the three stages of a river's journey?

What are some of the sources that start a river?

Name an animal that makes a journey from river to sea and back again?

What is a river delta?

Where is most of the world's fresh water?

Why are rivers important to people and animals?

Key words

Waterfall

A

Dam	**Delta**
Lake	**Mouth**
River	**Source**

Meander

Glossary

Dissolve – When a substance melts away and disappears when it is mixed in liquid.

Drought – When there is not enough rainfall and rivers and lakes dry up.

Erode – When something is worn away such as the rock at the bottom of a river.

Glacier – A river of ice that moves slowly down a valley.

Irrigation – When water is brought to crops to help them grow.

Microscopic – Something so tiny that it is only seen clearly through a microscope.

B

Pollution – Harmful chemicals, gases or rubbish that damage the environment.

Sediment – Tiny pieces of rock, soil and plants that are carried in river water.

Fresh waterways

Rivers and lakes are very important. Many living things, including people, would not be able to live without the fresh water in rivers and lakes. Rivers and lakes are part of the Earth's never-ending water cycle.

◀ ▲ **Rivers and lakes hold fresh water.**

A river is a large stream of fresh water that flows in a channel across the land. Every river changes the landscape it flows through. Lakes are large amounts of water that are enclosed by land on all sides. They form in hollows, craters or in dips in the land. The water in lakes is also fresh water.

Water is always being recycled.

Most of the world's water is salty sea-water (97 per cent), and the rest (three per cent) is fresh water. Most of the fresh water is frozen in the polar ice caps. Less than one per cent of the world's fresh water flows in rivers and lakes. This fresh water is constantly being recycled in the water cycle.

1 The Sun heats up sea-water. This turns it into **water vapour** which rises into the air.

5 Rivers carry the water to the sea. The water cycle starts all over again.

2 Winds carry the water vapour higher up and over the land. The water vapour cools and condenses into water droplets which form clouds.

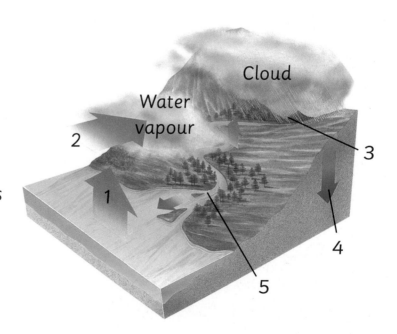

3 The water droplets fall as rain, hail or snow. This water falls as fresh water. It is not salty.

4 The water seeps into the ground and makes its way into streams and rivers.

 Can you find out the names of the different types of cloud?

A river's journey

Many rivers begin on high ground in the mountains where there is lots of rain and snow. Rivers always flow downhill towards flatter land. Then most rivers flow on until they reach the sea. Some rivers flow into lakes.

► **This stream begins at a spring, high up in the mountains.**

The place where a river begins is called its source. The source can be a spring or a melting **glacier**. It can also be rainwater collecting in low-lying places, a bog or a lake. The water from all these sources trickles downhill to form a stream. Tiny streams called **tributaries** join together as they rush downhill. As the streams join, the main stream gets bigger and wider and forms a river.

▲ **This young river flows down through a steep valley.**

A river's journey has different stages.

Geographers divide a river's journey into three stages. The beginning of a river, when it flows quickly with lots of energy, is called a young river. The middle of a river's journey, when it gets bigger and slows down, is called middle age. Finally, when the river reaches the end of its journey, it is called an old river.

As a young river flows quickly down a steep slope, it carves a channel into the landscape. The stones and gravel carried by the river rub on the river bed like sandpaper. They **erode** the river-bed and cut out a V-shaped river valley.

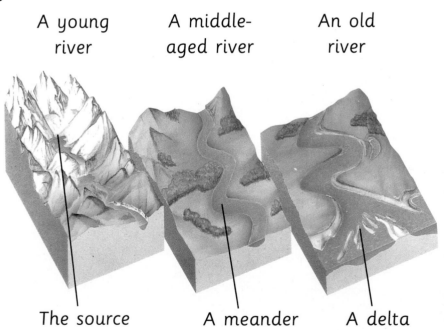

A young river
A middle-aged river
An old river

The source   A meander   A delta

 What makes young rivers flow so fast?

Slowing down

When a river reaches flatter land it becomes middle aged. The river is wider and flows more slowly through broad valleys. It carries a lot of mud, soil and sand which give the river water a muddy colour.

▶ **The river flows slowly in curves and bends across flatter land.**

The river now flows slowly along in great snake-like loops and curves called meanders. The flat land on each side of the river is called the flood plain. After heavy rain or snow melt, the level of the river may rise enough to spill over its banks and cover the flood plain.

◀ The soil near a river is very good for growing crops.

When rivers flood they leave behind a layer of rich **sediment** on the flood plain. This makes the soil fertile and excellent for growing crops. In Ancient Egypt the annual flooding of the River Nile gave the people a rich fertile soil so they could grow crops in the dry, barren desert.

Rivers can change direction.

The water flows fastest on the outside of a bend. This wears away the land and makes the curve bigger. The water flows slowest on the inside of a bend. Mud is dropped and builds up into new land. When a river is in flood it may cut across and take a faster course. This forms an oxbow lake.

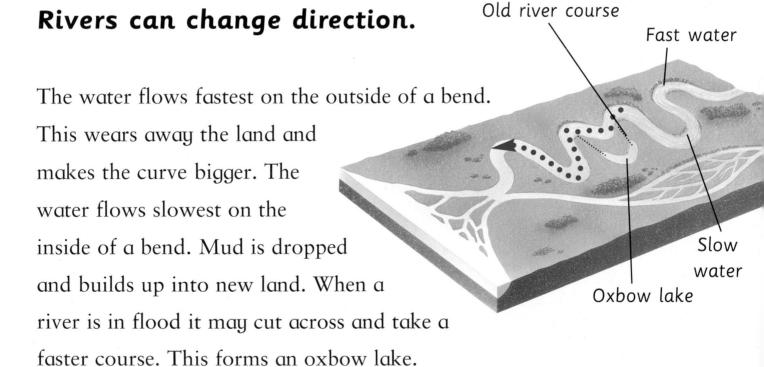

Old river course

Fast water

Slow water

Oxbow lake

 Why is a flood sometimes a good thing?

Meeting the sea

When a river nears the sea it widens out. At high tide the salty sea-water washes into the river. It mixes with the fresh water which is flowing into the sea. The place where the river flows into the sea is called the river's mouth.

◀ **Many birds feed on the mud flats at low tide.**

Some rivers' mouths widen out into a flat area called an estuary. The slow-flowing river drops its load of sediment which builds up into flat muddy areas called mud flats. The mud flats are important for wildlife. Wading birds come to the estuary to feed on animals living in the mud.

New land is made at the mouth of some rivers.

The sediment dropped in the mouth of large rivers can sometimes build up into new islands of land called a delta. Tiny pieces of mud are carried further out to sea, where they build up and add to the delta.

Tigers live at the mouth of the River Ganges.

The River Ganges flows through India and Bangladesh and has formed a delta in the Bay of Bengal. This delta is called the Sundarbans and is an important wildlife area. It is home to many rare animals such as crocodiles and Bengal tigers. The River Ganges delta is the largest delta in the world and is made up of more than fifty low islands.

 Why do birds come to mud flats?

Lakes

Lakes form in hollows in the land. Some, such as the Great Lakes in North America, were made by ice sheets carving the land. Other lakes form in the craters of old volcanoes or in cracks made by movements in the Earth's surface.

▶ **Lake Michigan is one of the five Great Lakes.**

The Great Lakes are enormous. They lie between Canada and the USA. The lakes are used for transporting goods and people. They also offer fishing, sailing and other water sports. Many big cities, such as Chicago (right), have grown up on their shores. **Pollution** from factories, shipping and cities has damaged parts of the lakes.

◀ Flamingos live and feed in soda lakes.

Most lakes contain fresh water, but some contain salty water. The water of Lake Magadi in Tanzania contains a mineral called soda. Not many animals can live in the water, but algae and shrimps thrive and these provide food for millions of flamingos.

This is the oldest and deepest lake in the world.

Lake Baikal in Russia is the world's deepest lake. It holds more water than all of the Great Lakes put together. Three quarters of the plants and animals that live there are found nowhere else. Lake Baikal is home to the world's only freshwater seal.

 Which other lakes can you name?

Powerful water

Rivers slowly wear away the land where they flow. They carry stones which rub and scrape against the river-bed. Pieces of loosened soil and rock are washed downstream. Over time, rivers make a deeper and wider channel.

► **Water can flow underground and carve out caves.**

In areas with limestone rock, water seeps underground through tiny holes in the rock. Because rainwater is slightly acidic, it **dissolves** the rock and makes the holes bigger. Gradually water carves out caves and tunnels. Underground rivers usually come to the surface through a spring or cave further downhill.

◀ The Grand Canyon was carved out by a river.

The Grand Canyon in the USA was carved out by the Colorado River. It is the deepest, widest and longest canyon in the world. The canyon has steep sides which were formed as the river cut down through the layers of hard rock.

This river pours over the edge of Niagara Falls.

When a river flows over hard rock with soft rock underneath, the soft rock is worn away more quickly than the hard rock. This leaves a shelf of hard rock. The river pours over this shelf and makes a waterfall. Eventually the hard rock shelf collapses and the waterfall moves upstream. Niagara Falls moves over a metre upstream every year.

Hard rock

Soft rock

 Can you find out which is the highest waterfall in the world?

Water wildlife

Rivers and lakes are home to many different animals. Some animals spend their whole lives in the water. Others live on land and visit the water to hunt, drink or breed. Frogs start their lives in water and then move onto land.

▶ **Otters live in some rivers.**

Animals that live in and around water may have specially adapted features to suit their habitat. The otter is a warm-blooded animal so it needs a fur coat to keep it warm in winter. Otters are sleek and streamlined, with a powerful tail and webbed feet. This makes them excellent swimmers.

▶ Salmon jump up waterfalls to reach their home rivers.

Baby salmon hatch out of eggs laid in gravel river-beds and spend the first year of their life in the nearest lake. Then they journey down river and into the sea. When adult salmon are ready to mate, they return to the place where they hatched. To get home, they must battle against the river's flow, strong currents, waterfalls and predators.

Larva

Dragonflies live in and out of the water.

Dragonflies spend most of their lives as larvae underwater. When a larva is ready to become an adult, it crawls out of the water onto a plant stem. Its skin splits and an adult dragonfly with wings emerges.

 How do webbed feet help an animal to swim?

Freshwater plants

The plants that grow in rivers and lakes are important. They provide homes and food for many animals. Underwater plants also release the gas oxygen, which underwater animals need to breathe.

◀ **Many animals like to eat these water plants. They are called algae.**

Some plants grow underwater. The simplest underwater plants are **microscopic** algae which are no bigger than a full-stop. They float freely in the water making it look green and slimy. Larger types of algae grow in a green fuzzy layer attached to rocks or on the surface of larger plants.

► The leaves of this giant water lily can grow up to two metres across.

Some plants have leaves and flowers that float on the surface. The giant Amazon water lily's roots are anchored in the river-bed, but its leaves float on the surface to catch sunlight. The underside of each leaf has air-filled ribs which support it and keep it afloat.

Reeds can make new land.

Plants that grow along lake shores or river-banks are called marginal plants. Marginals grow thickly and spread by sending roots through the mud. The roots trap sediment and can gradually turn a lake into land. The lake grows smaller and will eventually become land.

 Why are water plants so important to animal life?

Living by rivers and lakes

Everyone needs water to live. We need it to drink, cook and wash. For thousands of years people have settled and built their homes near rivers and lakes. Before roads and railways, people used rivers and lakes for travelling.

◀ **Rivers are used to carry goods.**

The River Rhine is the busiest water-way in Europe. It flows from Switzerland through Germany and The Netherlands to the huge port of Rotterdam and the North Sea. Tugs and barges carry steel, iron, petrol and timber along the River Rhine.

► Water from rivers and lakes helps crops to grow.

In many parts of the world, it is very hot and dry. Where there is not enough rainfall, farmers take water from rivers and lakes to **irrigate** their crops. They dig irrigation channels or ditches which bring water directly from the river to the fields.

These houses are built on stilts to keep them above the water.

Many people live close to rivers and lakes and use water plants as building materials.

These people have used reeds to build their houses.

 How do people make use of rivers and lakes?

Changing waterways

Many people and animals depend on rivers and lakes for their food and drink. Sometimes rivers and lakes change, are damaged or polluted. The people and wildlife that rely on them may have trouble finding clean water.

◄ **Rivers can spill over the river-banks and flood the land.**

After heavy rain, the level of a river can rise making it pour out over the flood plain. Fast-flowing flood water can sweep away everything in its path, causing damage to crops and homes, and killing people and animals. In some parts of the world, rivers flood every year.

◀ **This river is drying up because there has not been enough rain.**

During a **drought**, when there is much less rain than usual, rivers and lakes may dry up. This causes problems for people and wildlife who depend on the river or lake for water to drink or for watering crops.

These people are cleaning a lake that was damaged by rubbish.

Lakes and rivers can be damaged by **pollution**. Rubbish, sewage, pesticides, oil and fertilisers are often washed into the water. They can harm or kill the wildlife and plants, and change the delicate balance of the river or lake.

 What pollution have you seen in a river or lake?

Controlling the water

Rivers can be very powerful. We are learning how to control them and stop them causing flood damage. Rivers can be made safer to protect people and their homes. Controlling rivers can help guarantee that people always have enough water.

◀ **This barrier will protect the city of London from flooding.**

Engineers have designed the Thames Barrier, in London, to stop high surges of water flowing up the River Thames from the North Sea. The barrier is a 520-metre-wide wall of steel which can be raised when there is a flood alert. When it is not needed, the steel gates rest on the riverbed.

▶ Some people use rivers and lakes to have fun.

Some people spend their leisure time on or by rivers and lakes. Walkers and campers enjoy the natural surroundings. Others sail or go canoeing. White water rafting is popular on fast-flowing rivers. Some lake shores are used like beaches.

A man-made lake is created behind this dam.

Dams are built across rivers to control the flow of water. They can prevent flooding and give a constant and steady supply of water. The power of the water rushing through dams is often used to generate electricity. The Three Gorges Dam in China is the world's biggest dam. When it is completed in 2009, its reservoir will be more than 550 kilometres long.

Why do people try to control water?

Great rivers

There are different ways of measuring rivers. One way is to measure the length, from the source to the mouth. Rivers do not flow in straight lines, so all the curves must be measured. Another way is to measure the amount of water that flows in a river.

◀ The world's longest river, the Nile, flows through the desert.

The River Nile flows from the mountains near Lake Victoria in East Africa, northwards to the Mediterranean Sea. The water from the River Nile is used to grow crops in a green strip of land on either side of the river. It brings water to the hot, dry deserts of Egypt and Sudan. In Egypt, most people live on the fertile strip by the river.

▶ The Amazon River flows through hot tropical rainforest.

The mighty Amazon River is the world's second longest river but it carries more water than any other river. About one fifth of all the world's river water flows out of the Amazon into the Atlantic Ocean. It carries water across a huge area, from one side of South America to the other.

The Yangtze River is the third longest in the world.

River	Where is it found?	How long is it?
Nile	Africa	6,671 km
Amazon	South America	6,437 km
Yangtze	Asia	6,300 km
Huang He	Asia	5,463 km
Congo	Africa	4,375 km

 Why do people settle near rivers and lakes?

See how much you know!

What happens to lakes and rivers during a drought?

Can you name the three stages of a river's journey?

What are some of the sources that start a river?

Name an animal that makes a journey from river to sea and back again?

What is a river delta?

Where is most of the world's fresh water?

Why are rivers important to people and animals?

Key words

Waterfall

Dam   **Delta**   **Flood**

Lake   **Mouth** **Mud flat**

River   **Source** **Spring**

Stream **Valley**

Meander

Glossary

Dissolve – When a substance melts away and disappears when it is mixed in liquid.

Drought – When there is not enough rainfall, and rivers and lakes dry up.

Erode – When something is worn away such as the rock at the bottom of a river.

Glacier – A river of ice that moves slowly down a valley.

Irrigation – When water is brought to crops to help them grow.

Microscopic – Something so tiny that it is only seen clearly through a microscope.

Pollution – Harmful chemicals, gases or rubbish that damage the environment.

Sediment – Tiny pieces of rock, soil and plants that are carried in river water.

Tributary – A stream that flows into a larger stream or river.

Water vapour – Tiny droplets of water that float around in the air.

Index